STARTUP

The Complete Entrepreneur's Guide to Starting a Business

(How to Turbocharge Your Startup Growth Without Complicated Growth Hacks)

Michael Poole

Published By Jordan Levy

Michael Poole

All Rights Reserved

Startup: The Complete Entrepreneur's Guide to Starting a
Business (How to Turbocharge Your Startup Growth Without
Complicated Growth Hacks)

ISBN 978-1-77485-306-1

Legal & Disclaimer

The information contained in this book is not designed to replace or take the place of any form of medicine or professional medical advice. The information in this book has been provided for educational and entertainment purposes only.

The information contained in this book has been compiled from sources deemed reliable, and it is accurate to the best of the Author's knowledge; however, the Author cannot guarantee its accuracy and validity and cannot be held liable for any errors or omissions. Changes are periodically made to this book. You must consult your doctor or get professional medical advice before using any of the suggested remedies, techniques, or information in this book.

Upon using the information contained in this book, you agree to hold harmless the Author from and against any damages, costs, and expenses, including any legal fees potentially resulting from the application of any of the information provided by this guide. This disclaimer applies to any damages or injury caused by the use and application, whether directly or indirectly, of any advice or information presented, whether for breach of contract, tort, negligence, personal injury, criminal intent, or under any other cause of action.

You agree to accept all risks of using the information presented inside this book. You need to consult a professional medical practitioner in order to ensure you are both able and healthy enough to participate in this program.

TABLE OF CONTENTS

Introduction

You have an excellent idea for your new venture or you are trying to find the perfect business that will work for you. You've made the right choice in buying this book. A lot of people don't have the time or energy to research the right thing they're doing which is the reason why many startups fail. It's better to think about and know what you're getting yourself into instead of entering the wilderness without a plan.

If a company is new, it is offering the market with a brand-new product or service, or it offers an existing service or product in a novel method. Startups are able to turn into extremely profitable businesses, but they also carry a high risk due to the fact that when you present new ideas to the marketplace, there is no way to gauge its success until the product is released and evaluates the market. In the beginning, founder(s) of the venture typically begin to run the business alone until it's time to grow and recruit additional team members to handle the business so that the founders are able to focus in the business, not working in the business.

While starting a business is risky and difficult to manage If done in the right way could open the possibility of huge success as well as the possibility to become your own boss. Startups can begin at home or with you and your friends, and soon become an established name within its field. Startups are popping up every day. Some of the latest or most recently-launched startups rapidly gaining traction are DropBox, AirBnB and SnapChat and many others that you're likely already familiar with because of their success.

Although these examples may be as successful as they are, starting a new business which is successful later on isn't easy.

Within this guide, you'll discover the best ways to cover all your bases and go about it correctly when you launch an enterprise of your own. Since startups tend to be extremely risky, you'll need to learn how to set up your business properly the first time to avoid making the same mistakes that tens of thousands of others have made before you.

In the next pages, you will discover how to design a startup that has the greatest chances of success. Learn the definition of an entrepreneur who is a startup and how you can use specific strategies, abilities and practices to conduct business correctly first time around. Learn how to think of and research a good startup concept if you haven't previously done so. Then, you will discover the most effective ways to bring your concept to fruition as a successful company that is profitable and sustainable.

Chapter 1: What it takes to Start A Coaching Business Online And Not Have Just A Job as a Coach

If you visit a variant of an Coaching Institute or a Coaching School or an Coaching Certification Program If you are spending the time chatting to an audience of speakers from the National Speakers Association, you will encounter a culture of dollars-for-hours. There will be discussions about the possibility of charging $50 per hour, starting at $50 per hour to $100 an hour and so on.

The entire society is likely to revolve around exchange of time to earn money.

There are many issues in that.

The problem with this is the fact that your time is limited. Even if you discover the means to work all hours of the day as a coach for 50 dollars per hour, you'll only make $1200 a day, and there's no way to earn more since the time you have available is limited.

If there's no way to create more progress, no more future, there is no growth, no improvement most people become bored at any job. In the end, it happens to everyone.

In the end, every lawyer who is charged per hour, every psychologist, and each CPA is not going to be a lawyer psychologist or CPA. They are stuck, and that's the situation you'll face as well in the event that you charge by hour.

It is therefore impossible to make substantial profits by charging per hour , and it's equally impossible to achieve significant growth.

Another issue with the charging per hour model is that it's not the case for a business. It's a job which does not have leverage. It does not have a multiplier effect.

In this book, we'll discuss coaching online as a business that allows you to charge clients not by hour, but instead per project or value you provide to your client.

Here's how you should think about coaching and what value the coach offers If you visit the therapist who saves a marriage, what do you think it is worth? What is the amount two individuals save by not having to go through a divorce without getting their lives turned upside down?

It is not a good idea to compare a coach with someone else who is an hourly wage. Always try to look at the bigger picture because you'll be able charge more and will be able to assist people to achieve their goals.

A coach is not hired for the reason that they would like to pay $X/hour for coaching. The majority of people hire a coach an therapist, or a consultant in business to help them to get certain results. This is what you should be talking about, and that's the type of thing you're thinking about when you are pricing your services.

Another reason to not charge per hour is simple: if you cost per hour, everybody is dissatisfied.

We have discussed the reasons you'll be dissatisfied. Your clients will also be to be disappointed. They'll feel that they're overpaying for your services since they'll be viewing your services as a trade of dollars in exchange for the time you spend, if you permit them to see your services on an hourly basis.

They'll talk to you and think: "I am paying this person $500 per hour and we've talked in 30 minutes. I paid him $250. Was there enough value to me in that thirty minutes that I was worth the cost of $250?"

This is what happens when you charge per hour and not solely based on "saving the marriage."

In order to become a great coach, you must to let go of this old way of thinking in as many ways as you are able to.

What is the cost for coaching?

One of them is cash above the base. Let me describe how it operates. You have a conversation with a potential client and ask: "Okay, how much did you make in the last year?"

Let's suppose that your possible client earns $100,000 for the ease of argument. Let's say you have a rate of inflation is 10% and the growth rate of the company is another 10%..

This means that, this year, without your assistance and everything working the way that this potential client has done before, the client will earn $120,000. This will be the minimum for the initial year.

Base for the next year is calculated similarly. Let's assume one hundred thousand dollars for second, and $168,000 for the third .

As a coach, you may say that you will assist in the growth of the company and for compensation, you'll need 30% of the earnings that the company earns above the amounts mentioned above.

You could then convince someone that you're truly skilled and increase the revenue to $500,000 within the first year. That means that you'll receive one-third from (500-120)/3 equals $125,000. You can then reduce this by persuading your potential client to pay for example, $10,000 of this amount in advance.

The numbers we've used in this instance aren't that important. The most important thing is that we've shown how you can stay free from talking about hours for dollars in the coaching industry.

What you're currently planning to offer in this case isn't important. Your clients can't start counting their minutes and figure out what they're paying excessively per minute. The only thing important in the above-mentioned coaching program is the expansion of the company.

The other thing that the majority of Coaching Universities obsess about is formal education.

This is simple to comprehend as formal training is what they're selling. They're all about education, qualifications, credentials, and alphabet soup following the name. They'll tell you that there is no way to operate as an internet-based coach without letters following your name. However, in reality, this does not correspond with the reality.

It is vital to realize that no one really cares about the letters following your name, except for the institutions selling letters, as well as those who purchased the letters.

The market isn't concerned. Today , we live in a celebrity-driven society but not an expertise-driven culture.

The schooled experts made great money in the 30s and 40s of years ago. The people who are making high amounts of money today are known as celebrities.

Here's a concrete example to clearly illustrate this.

When you've got two fitness trainers who each have earned a degree from Harvard and has all the alphabet letters that go with the name of his/hers you could think of and the other is a trainer of Kim Kardashian, more people are choosing one of the Kim Kardashian guy versus the Harvard guy.

The misconceptions of formal training also manifest in the ladder of thinking. The ladder approach is crucial because it's what you want all others around you think.

As we get older it's our parents who decide when we're old enough to be able to look after our siblings, select your own clothing, and date. After that, we attend school , where there are grades. One is not allowed to go up to grade five until after the age of two.

It's the only method to get there is one or two, three, and then on. It's the ladder. Ladders are all over the world. We're taught to think of ladders in terms of.

The truth is that climbing up the ladders isn't the way life is for the majority of successful people. Bill Gates, Mark Zuckerberg, Steve Jobs dropped out of college. They didn't wait around until they had finished climbing the ladder to graduate.

They also didn't have anyone appointed to establish their companies. They've decided to do it because they've chosen to go ahead.

This is a model that you can follow:

Stop climbing ladders made by others.

Make the choices you choose to do when you make the decision to do them.

In the same way you don't want to change the thoughts of those who are around you. To change someone's way of thinking they think is difficult and ungrateful work. This isn't the kind of work you're supposed to be doing.

The formula for successful online coaching lies in the following:

Do not climb ladders constructed by others. Build your own ladders for others to climb.

It is important to stick ladders before your potential customers and customers. Once they have climbed an incline, you'll need to put another directly ahead of them because they'll be able to climb it. This is what we've all been taught to do.

However, it's essential not to climb a ladder. If someone hands you an unfinished ladder, it's best to be astonished. You must realize that a lot of people just like you sat in a room , and worked out how to build another ladder.

Boy Scouts of America has an ladder. Many people came to work in the same room to figure out the best way to build one to regulate children and parents. There's no better reason than this ladder to be in place.

Beware: if you do manage to get all your Coach University Certification Thinking out of your head, those who are from Coach

University are not going to be thrilled about it.

The people around you who are charging per hour for dollars aren't going to be thrilled to see you earning more than they're making.

How can you possibly take this kind of charge?

This is what you'll hear from them, and this is how you can tell if you're doing things right.

There is a constant debate within the American society regarding the difference between the normal Joy the pay of workers and the CEO's salary. Many find it incredibly unfair that a CEO could be earning 100x, 1000x, or 10000x the amount that the lowest-paid worker in the company earns.

What they aren't paying focus on is the differences between their skills and responsibilities. A few words from the CEO's mouth of the largest multinational corporation can yield billions of dollars of profits. What is the significance of those few words? What is the best way to measure it?

Consider this as the job of someone who cleans the floors. There's nothing they do that has similar effects on the business. Nothing can be compared to the situation in the above.

Even today, there are those who believe there must be some kind of artificial number that governs the differences between the wages of a cleaner for toilets and the CEO of a company.

For instance for a janitor earning $10/hour, the company claims that it should be multiplied by 18, say 18 times.

And nobody in the business is allowed to earn more than $180/hour.

This is not a new idea. It's been happening since the beginning of the industrial revolution. People used to say the same remarks regarding Andrew Carnegie and Henry Ford the way they do today concerning Bill Gates and Mark Zuckerberg.

They all have the same method in their minds when it comes down to coaching online. One of the most important aspects to remember is that there's no logic to this.

A lawyer is charged X dollars per hour, and the coach shouldn't charge more than Y for an hour.

The amount you pay as a coach ought to base it on a mix of value that is actually realized as determined and not by yourself, but rather by your clients, and the amount you are able to earn.

The two things which matter and ought to pay attention to.

Chapter 2: Most Effective Way to

Create Wealth

Many people imagine being wealthy. Actually, the majority all of our wealth in the world is ruled by just one percent from the total population. However, the chances are not very high that one will be able to achieve the life-changing wealth required to purchase extravagant cars, million-dollar homes, and costly jewellery as well as other items. Your search for ways to boost income is the best start.

I have studied a lot of people who have created wealth in the first generation I am of the conviction that becoming wealthy isn't as easy as studying a book as well as investing money in trading on the Forex market. However, having a company as an asset could eventually generate the income required and leverage to build wealth over your lifetime. Here's the best part - your company is able to create books, write books, or invest in Forex or many other things.

With regards to the possibilities you have when it comes to running a business, the sky truly is the limit!

Many people think that it is only possible to succeed in business by having a massive bank account, top-of-the-line connections, or even an undiscovered information source to begin with. What they aren't aware of is that everything begins somewhere and that some things can start with a humble foundation. It is best to begin your company from where you are at the moment.

One thing that all wealthy people share is the perseverance and determination to continue to work hard during the tough times.

Let's suppose you require $10,000 to start an online clothing shop and you only have $2,000 and an annual marketing budget between $500 and $1,000.

If you could find a landlord willing to offer you the rental for one month, and you found an agent to stock the shop, you'd be left with an extremely short amount of time to generate enough revenue to keep the shop running. The risk of failing or any unplanned expense ending to ruin your business is the biggest chance.

Today, the choice that most people choose is to hold on to their job and be angry in the event of being dismissed or one of a variety of events that result in them being in financial trouble.

Let's consider another possibility using the $2,000 to create a website that will drop ship the clothing line of your distributor and offering your clothing lines, or selling products from other companies and receiving an affiliate commission or a combination of these three.

It's difficult to recruit others online and make the most from them, especially if you're new to online business However, don't worry further, in this guide I'll offer tips and alternatives.

Focusing on what could happen when you've got your fully functioning web-based business are able to make use of the $500 per month to advertise your website, and as you develop the business , you'll be able to discover more. When you achieve more success , you can increase your earnings and start an offline business.

Working for a business vs. owning one for Others People

A lot of college and university students are going to tell that they're no anymore looking forward to securing an employment after they graduate. In reality, excellent jobs are becoming difficult to find because there are more job seekers nowadays than the amount of open jobs. Employers, you'll need to work harder to earn a little less than you did in the past market.

The amount you earn for your boss cannot be compared with the amount they pay you. They must leverage your efforts to get maximum value from their investment. When you work for someone else, the earnings you earn are not as high regardless of the hard work that you put into each day. In addition, even if are offered a job paying well, the workload will be so heavy that you won't have the time to devote to your family. Also, your schedule is likely to be in chaos.

In regards to their working lives, they typically don't plan the time required to go to work and get home after work. They also neglect other aspects like winding down after working all day or waking up early to make it to work in time. The 40-hour workweek is not true when you consider the overall consequences of having a "JOB".

The secret to making money by owning an enterprise is simple to attain by using these suggestions:

Even with the expense you'll incur however, you won't share the profits with anyone else.

Your earnings have every chance to grow with a greater return than if they are left unattended in an account in a bank.

The effect of hiring employees to help grow your business is difficult to measure.

Ten people working 40 hours a week equals 400 hours of your own work

Most people stay away from this route because they fear being unsuccessful or having to step out of their comfortable zone.

If you are a business proprietor,, your task is to identify opportunities that will pay you a higher return per hour than what you pay your employees. For instance, if you own an enterprise that earns you $20 per hour, and pay employees $10 per hour, then 40 hours you leveraged hours yields $4000 per week based on previous details mentioned above.

No matter how big the business earns more money if its expenses do not exceed the income generated.

If you take this into consideration and the other factors, you will also be able to see the fact that online businesses are not limited to time and can grow in value depending on the amount of the amount of traffic. Let me elaborate more, online you are not subject to no restrictions on space, just similar to the 1500 square feet of space in a mall. As hard as you try, you aren't able to put more items in your store, or keep it remain open past the hours that the store is opened. But online you can expand your inventory as high and wide as your hosting will allow and it's very simple to expand your online presence. We must not forget about the benefits of being accessible all day seven days a week as well as expanding to other countries with just one domain.

Start a new online clothing store such as Klothh.com. The approach to use social media in conjunction with constantly growing the base of their customers at the very least every month - could propel their business online to heights previously only achievable by the big box store's offline.

Even a service-based business such as My USA media group with MyUSAMediaGroup.com or MyUSALocal.com websites could provide similar products to different clients and consequently offer what each segment of business growth industry is seeking. Before the age of the internet it was necessary open two separate PR companies and pay double the cost while possibly alienating certain markets or.

No interruptions

Being an entrepreneur means that your objectives are more clear than when you are employed by others. If you're employed, you are able to work hard to achieve the goals that benefit those who run the company. It can be difficult to concentrate on your goals for yourself when employed by someone else because lots of your time is wasted as you shift from one employer to the next in search of more money.

When you work for yourself, you are your own boss and therefore, no one is able to remove you from the job. You can work whenever you'd like instead of being compelled to. If you are disciplined and determined you can build sustainable prosperity as you invest in your business and yourself.

The primary goal of any business is to earn income and to increase your chances to offer products or services to those who have enough value enough to pay for these products and services.

"Take one idea. It's your whole life. Think of it, think about it, fantasize about it, and then live with the idea. Allow your muscles, brain, nerves, and every part of your body be filled with the idea and let all other thoughts to the side. This is how you can achieve success." -- Swami Vivekananda

What would Warren Buffet Do?

By forming a virtual Master-mind group that includes the best business minds on the planet I'm able to get amazing results on a small budget. These contacts are useful as references in stressful situations. I would suggest everyone create an inventory of contacts that are present and former that you would like to talk to in the event of a crisis.

Imagine fantasy football, but focus on your business and a Dream Team!

This chapter is been a very special memory within my soul. The ideas came about through studying the idioms, idioms, and wise advice of one of the most successful investors of our time and perhaps the greatest investor of the past Warren Buffet. Warren Buffet the oracle of Omaha.

Knowing what to look out for in an investment is the best alternative to studying all of his books and having a million dollars meeting with the famous investor, before asking the most important question:

"What should I be looking for when investing in any company?"

"You don't have to be an expert in rocket science. It's not a contest where the person who has 160 IQ outperforms the person who has 130IQ." Warren Buffett

If you are looking for an investment that is suitable for you, taking ownership in a company or in a company is easy to achieve if you adhere to the basics and stick to the basics.

Do you know the business model you want to establish?

Does the business seem logical to you?

Would you consider selling the item or service to your mother?

In lieu of being focused on market trends instead, they focused on identifying long-term value. This is called fundamental analysis.

Are you sure that the company is sustainable or is it something that has a an expiration date?

Although a product may have a shelf-life that is limited and be subject to seasonality, your company is expected to be operational for long periods of time. It is costly to stop and begin an entirely new service or business following the marketing and promotion during tough times is not logical and could be harmful to maintaining the momentum required to reach higher levels of achievement.

When online my primary business is the creation of content. The need for quality content is essential in today's information age and will continue to be so 100 years down the road and beyond. Based on this, my company was built with a base which is built to last for whatever the circumstances.

"I am trying to purchase stock in companies that are so great that even a fool could manage them. For the simple

reason that sooner or later someone will."
Warren Buffett

However advanced and technologically
sophisticated a business may be, it must
be able to use processes and systems that
enable it to be managed and easy to
manage. How many steps will it need to
complete to get the final outcome? What
steps step-by-step are required to
accomplish the task?

McDonald's which, in my opinion is the
perfect model. While I've never cooked
the Big Mac, within just two hours, I can
take a seat and follow the instructions
they taught me and serve customers with
a meal. The more you can take your time
and break big tasks down into small steps
procedures and systems, the more
efficiently your business will function and
allow you to employ people and leverage

your system into a larger business once you're at the right time.

"I am more successful as an investor due to my status as a businessman and a better businessman as I'm not an investor."

Many business owners contact me for help and develop their online systems in order to promote and market their business on the web. Every time, they ask "How did you learn the details of my business... Is it because you probably studied or run the same type of business before?"

In reality, I'm a professional who knows how to build a company from scratch. I follow a structured strategy to incorporate the most essential elements of the process into methods that are later utilized to create more than a site. This gives us an advantage edge when working with more advanced clients.

Whatever business it is, it must maintain and/or grow its market share businesses that are smart recognize this and are able to grow large by investing in fundamentals of business.

It's surprising how many people destroy their businesses by adopting an Investor mentality of instant gratification and going for ideas that can bring them wealth, instead of investing time and again in the fundamental and often easy business building methods that will ensure their success.

I invite anyone in business to discuss their business with the team I work with, and within 24 hours, we will have a clear idea of at a minimum, a bullet-point strategy to optimize the company to grow and achieve greater performance.

It doesn't matter what type of company you run, if it sells any item or service to customers, it is possible to optimize and enhanced through our strategies techniques, processes, and strategies. A lot of these are discussed in this particular book.

If I had one million dollars today, or even $10 million in the future I'd be investing 100. Anyone who says that the size doesn't affect investment performance is lying. The highest returns I've had were back in 1950s. I wiped out the Dow. You should look at the numbers. It was a bit of a gamble back at the time. It's an enormous benefit not to own an excessive amount of money. I believe I could earn you 50% per year for one million dollars. But I'm sure I could. I can assure you that.

A lot of money can take away the ability to be agile as well as thinking in the manner of a startup investing all your energy into something or feeling hungry. Certain situations lend themselves more to David rather than Goliath.

When I began my Internet business, I had plenty of cash from previous investments in real estate. My success on the internet was a result of burning through the majority of my other resources and almost failing my new business.

It was a transition from feeling huge in my own mind and euphoric about my own achievements to being back to the passion and determination that I needed to keep going with the goals! What you see becoming bigger and bigger was the result of having a focus and pushing myself up to the ceiling.

Absolutely not! I am not advocating that anyone with a lot of funds should invest it all in any company. It is not advisable to do so before conducting tests to scale, and being confident that they have a successful business model.

Rule No.1: Never lose money. Rule No.2: Never forget rule No.1.

The strategy and approach are very similar , in that you take in every bit of information you can and continue building up that foundation of knowledge as new facts change. You take whatever probabilities are suggested based on the information of your current time, however, you're always prepared to alter your actions or approach when you learn new information.

We do not want to rely on the generosity of strangers to fulfill our obligations for tomorrow.

I constantly consider how quickly I can recover the capital investment. This is critical to consider when investing in new ventures. Knowing what you need to generate at the very least the amount of money you're making, then you will be able to make an informed choice if you want to make a commitment.

The more proficient you are with managing your money, the less likely to fail when creating your own company or buying a business you have purchased.

When it comes to managing your investment and business finances effectively, nothing is more beneficial to your bottom line than these spreadsheets that are easy to use:

1.) Bookkeeping Spreadsheet Your financial records are essential!

2.) Profit and Loss Statement (also known as a profit and loss statement) - Costs, revenue and expenses over the specified time.

3.) Cash-flow Statement: See the way that changes to the balance sheet and income impact your earnings.

The bloodline of income is vital to any business that is successful. Having these spreadsheets available is similar to having the ability to track the condition of your body through health checks and doctor appointments.

These "real figures" are invaluable to make decisions and plan to achieve more results.

"Only purchase something that you'd happily hold even if the market closed down for 10 years." -- Warren Buffett

Chapter 3: Additional Vital Tips for

Startups to Consider

With the resources needed to start your own company at the start and grow it into a lasting enterprise, it's important to stick to an established business plan. The way they describe it is "don't change an effective team" This also applies to businesses. You shouldn't alter a successful business structure. Should you change it, you risk the risk losing the trust of your customers, as well as your part of market share. Here are some helpful tips that will help you start your own business and help it grow into a thriving business;

Tip #1: Use as many marketing and technology tools as you can.

If you're an entrepreneur you have access to a broad selection of tools and applications you can employ to advertise your company online. There are numerous applications, in addition to tools for business improvement that are accessible for free on computers, tablets and even smartphones. Use these apps to market your business to potential customers.

Tip #2: Increase the size of your business by utilizing SEO (Search engine Optimization (SEO)

No matter if your business startup is online-based or not, it is essential to employ basic and sophisticated SEO strategies to bring it on the top of the search engines like Google. Simple SEO strategies include keyword-rich content linking, a good web designs that are navigable easily through by internet users. Do your best to connect your content with other blogs and websites that rank high as this is one of the most effective ways to promote your brand's name across multiple channels. Be sure to write informative articles that benefit your readers on an ongoing basis and will make them be drawn back to your site.

Tips #3: Increase sales by using social media

Social media is the single most powerful marketing and promotion instrument in the world in the present. The number of people who sign to Top social media sites, including Facebook, Twitter, Pinterest, Instagram, and LinkedIn regularly has grown and these networks can expose your business to millions of users on a regular basis. The best thing about using social media for marketing tool is that it's accessible for free and you are able to create as numerous groups as you like.

Although the usage of social media is totally free, it is important to ensure that your followers are with you. Do your best to share relevant and positive material on your Facebook and Twitter accounts frequently, and also make every effort to reply to comments since they are crucial to the success of your business. Choose those who are the most active followers of your group since they could be your business leads.

Tip #4: Create an effective support system

Your entrepreneurial journey could seem like a lonely journey, but it's not. Prior to launching your first venture, you have to ensure that you're supported by the appropriate people, such as your family and friends as well as your colleagues, friends even your investors. It is essential to have the psychological and emotional support from these people They may not all offer the financial backing you need, however there is a wealth of good suggestions you can obtain from these people.

Tip #5: React to any feedback you receive and improve your initial model

Feedback can help your business expand and grow. The more positively you receive these, the more improving or fine-tuning you could make to increase the value of your company. Since genuine feedback is not sought, but you should allow your customers to share their opinions about your services and products and then use that feedback to improve the quality of your product.

Chapter 4: The Way to Develop a

Good Communication

Entrepreneurs interact with their customers on a regular basis. It is essential to communicate with your investors, suppliers employees, customers, and employees. Therefore, you must have exceptional communication skills if wish to excel in the business world.

Within this section, you'll discover five methods that can aid you in improving your communication abilities.

A Professional's Idea

Marc Benioff, the founder and CEO of Salesforce.com created the company with a billion dollars by telling great stories. He imagined new ideas to satisfy the requirements of prospective customers. Then, he transformed his ideas into products that his customers could purchase. The most significant aspect of his mission was, however, the sharing his ideas with others. He utilized his skills in communication and interpersonal to persuade clients. In the course of an interview declared"communication is by far the most essential element of becoming an businessman.

If you're looking to become successful, you must improve your communication abilities. Remember that even the best products will not help when you aren't able to communicate with your clients.

The Techniques

Three strategies you should employ to increase your communication abilities:

Respond immediately to others Set a timer that you respond to any demands immediately, within 24 hours. The ability to respond is crucial for the growth of every business owner. If you wish for your business to thrive and expand then you must be responsive to your customers as well as your employees, investors and suppliers as quickly as time you can. This method also shows your customers that you appreciate your time.

Utilize the social Networking Sites - To be a successful communicator, it is essential to be able to communicate with others using any of the channels. Today the most popular channels for communication are email as well as social networks. Today's customers prefer social media for getting in touch with businesses due to the fact the channel is personalized and offers immediate communications.

Create Great Stories - Stories appeal to the reader's emotions. Since the majority of customers make use of their emotions when deciding on products and services, you must be able to craft and communicate powerful stories. Your company's mission and past achievements when speaking to your clients.

Be confident - The best people communicate with confidence, even when they're anxious. So, you must appear confident when you interact with others. Make use of the body language and facial expressions to show confidence. According to studies of recent times over 60 percent of the impression people get about their speakers is determined by those two elements.

Develop a strong presentation skills - As the founder of a new business you represent your company's image. People will form opinions about your business through the way they interact. Therefore, you need to master the art of giving impressive presentations. It is important to convey your thoughts and ideas with the highest quality possible. So, the public will be impressed with your company.

Chapter 5: Getting Started

You should be able to determine the kind of business you'd like to explore based on your own individual interests as well as the competitive landscape. When you're considering creating a fresh product, or selling specific products to a certain segment of your audience it is important to think about which sources to use for the products that you'll eventually sell.

Take a look at the type of seller you will encounter.

If you want to determine if your business is feasible, take a examine local producers as well as international ones. Utilizing locally-sourced products generally is simpler and you can sell products made locally, however, the extra cost associated with this strategy are too high for companies that face stiff competition in cost.

This isn't always a definite norm, however. If you're dealing with fragile items, local shipping can offer more protection in the event that items arrive damaged frequently. Costs can be determined by researching manufacturing process as well as the shipping in order to calculate the basic price of your product.

Dropshipping: You do not have to be concerned about keeping any inventory of actual products offering the correct products. This method of fulfillment is referred to as dropshipping. it is a method that allows a vendor to purchase items direct from the producer (or an additional third company) and then delivers the products to customers directly. This assigns the vendor the responsibility of managing sales, customer service and retention of customers. The profits generated by dropshipping can be less than other kinds of business options however, the initial cost is significantly lower and the initial investment is virtually absent.

The most significant issue is a poor vendor who makes you face problems that are beyond your control. So pick your vendor carefully. In addition, handling the return process in this case is difficult, since you need to address the issue of the customer and the vendor must negotiate an agreement, which can lead to numerous unnecessary problems.

If you are interested in the concept that someone else handles the logistics of shipping and storage, and you are selling a product made locally or that you source your own, you can try to use the

Fulfilment by Amazon program. It's among the easiest methods to begin. This program allows customers to set up their own Amazon store and then stock it with whatever they like prior to transferring the products to Amazon to keep until they are sold. Amazon will then take care of customer service, shipping and returns and more and all you need to do is provide them with a the appropriate percentage of each goal and then pay them twice each month.

The greatest benefit of this Fulfilment by Amazon program is that as you are a member, all your purchases will be eligible for free two-day shipping via Amazon Prime. Since Amazon Prime users are always trying to cut down the costs associated with this service, they will almost always opt for a product with this feature, instead of another similar option regardless of whether it's the most expensive one of the two. Once you have this set up it is possible to have a website to run like normal, but instead of a store , you will have a page which links back to your Amazon site directly.

This approach has the advantage of permitting Amazon to perform the majority of the logistical lifting but at the same time giving you the ability to set up your own website and to market your products. This can reduce your margins for profit however, as Amazon will take a percentage of every sale.

Locating a reliable vendor: You might prefer dealing with a vendor face-to-face. If this is the case, keep an eye out for local wholesalers or craftsman tradeshows within a short drive from your residence. Tradeshows give you the chance to interact with vendors in an environment that works in your favor. In addition, you can meet a variety of wholesalers over a brief period of time, but having all of them in the same space virtually guarantee you the best price as your desire to beat the competition is real.

The cost of local vendors are likely to be higher than those of a business located overseas. Being capable of interacting with someone directly (especially beginning out) can eliminate the problem of trust completely. This can be a relief for those who are just starting their business from beginning from scratch. It's more likely that you will find lower costs at a local tradeshow rather than local wholesale suppliers since the majority of these sites purchase wholesale from real vendors and mark their goods at 20 percent, then market them under their own brand.

International sourcing: If have the funds to fund your idea from the very beginning in large quantities, you'll always get cheaper prices when outsourcing manufacturing requirements to out of the country. The hurdle to entry in projects like this can be high, but the advantages of outsourcing are twofold. Your costs will are lower, but , most important, handling these issues directly lets you be competitive at a level that your competitors who went the easy way will not be able to beat.

Begin your search by visiting Alibab.com for suppliers in the overseas market. This is an online catalog website that offers a range of Asian producers. While you can get good bargains when you buy in bulk, it is not the primary goal. Utilize this info to find manufacturers directly.

Take into consideration the ease your product will get through customs when dealing with foreign sellers. It is essential to consider all aspects of the product that you are considering, and then take your time as certain items may be delay (the list is lengthy and quite surprising). If you think it's possible that your product could delay for any reason, return to the drawing boards as it's too risky to take on.

Another issue to deal against is the barrier to communication, unless you're able to communicate in the official language of the company you're working with. A lot of countries in the world offer English but that doesn't mean that it is easy to talk on the phone. It is possible to communicate better by email. It is essential to go slow in this process since you're not getting any where if you are impatient, and the result will be enough to compensate for it, if you are careful.

If you manage to get through the entire negotiation process successfully, ensure that you are studying the contract thoroughly to ensure you know that nothing has changed. The nature of negotiations is more flexible in certain regions of the world. If you don't point out the errors before signing the agreement it's likely that the dispute will be resolved to your advantage.

In the end, it is crucial to establish a timeline that allows you to return at the very least two shipments of defects before you finish having something that is usable even if it's not custom-made to order. Although it is highly unlikely that two orders that are complete are unusable, it's likely that there is some work to be done in order to reach an acceptable level of consistency you're comfortable with.

If you find an organization that can to meet your requirements in a reasonable manner it is essential that you do everything can to help ensure that the relationship is as solid as you can. Stay in contact with your sales representative on a regular basis even if you're not placing an order. Your aim should be to be a part of the lives of your counterparts to ensure that should they quit the company, you're not left in the cold and compelled to repeat the whole process all over again. As with everything else, finding items from outside of the country is all about the people you know. Once you've found a reliable and trustworthy supplier Do everything you can to make the customers happy.

The choice of how you show your online identity

There are many online sales platforms that you can choose from. Based on the product you sell and the source of it, is a crucial factor to consider. The eCommerce partner may be accountable for as high as

90% of the experience users have on your website. So, making a poor choice at this moment could have a direct impact on the future of your future business.

There are a few fundamental requirements to choose the best e-commerce partner . Choose if you want to build your own store online or want to utilize an existing. Although a customized store may cost more upfront however, it will give customers a unique experience customers, and you will be in total control over.

However in the event that you're not linked to an e-commerce marketplace , you'll naturally be more struggling with developing a base of customers regardless of the good quality or value of what that you offer. It is crucial to keep in mind that you'll make more profit when you run the business on your own, because you don't have to donate a portion of your profits to a third-party. It is possible to think of the differences between the possibility of owning an online storefront (your own website) as opposed to renting space in an outlet mall (working with the marketplace).

If you choose to build your own online store by hand, the next step to decide is whether you want to run your own software for point of sale and having another person handle the job for you. Although hosting everything yourself gives you more control, but it's also a lot more complex and has the possibility of leaving you vulnerable to legal action if the information on your website is taken by hackers. In general If you're not an experienced expert within the internet sector, then let this portion in the procedure to processionals.

If you decide instead to join a reputable marketplace like Etsy, eBay or Amazon You will have less work to accomplish in the beginning since the restrictions placed on your personal web space are more streamlined than they are otherwise. Furthermore, you don't need to think about creating advertising from scratch as millions of users are using these sites each day. Instead, the main task you'll have to complete is to get your product in the system.

Make sure that your choice is not mutually exclusive and using a third-party platform to establish a name and reputation for yourself is a good option. This puts your brand out in front of the masses at the speed that is most convenient, with the added benefit of being able to increase the trust of customers to your company. Once you've built up an audience that is loyal and have a loyal following, you can launch independently.

Think about your options: While browsing through the many e-commerce platforms available, be aware that there's not a single platform that is superior to all the other platforms. The best e-commerce platform is one which best suits your requirements.

Learn about the top names within the industry and also Gumroad in case you plan to market digital content or NuOrder in the event that you want to market a product to other companies directly. If you're looking to take pre-orders for a custom-made product then look into Celery.com.

No matter which option you select regardless of your choice, you must thoroughly explore your options to ensure that your store is the most unique it can be. This is especially important when the market you've selected is full of products similar to what you plan to sell. In the end, it is crucial that your marketplace is compatible with as many kinds of devices as you can.

It is essential to examine all services offered which include things like analytics reports, customer service accounting, shipping, ordering, etc., when exploring specific markets. It is important to examine the design of the website using a conventional computer as well as a mobile device. Additionally, markets of all kinds are shifting towards niches that is why you must conduct some study to find out if the extent to which your product(s) and services align with these directions.

Ideas for creating your own website If you do not want to be part of an online marketplace however in the same way, you aren't keen on coding your own site from the starting point The best option is to look into the e-commerce platforms that are self-hosted, which means you lease an area from the company, then add your own content and fully control the space.

It means that you'll be the processing of credit cards, which is why it's essential to ensure that the platform you choose is compliant to all payments laws governing the industry of cards. If you do not, you could land the company into hot waters in the future. The best method to avoid having to go through the specifics of this is to make all your transactions through PayPal.

Chapter 6: Different Types Of

Metrics

There are two kinds of metrics that you can employ when conducting Lean Analytics. They are qualitative and quantitative metrics. For starters, qualitative indicates that the metric is in close relationship with your clients. This includes things like feedback or interviews. This will provide you with a detailed understanding of the metrics.

There is also the option of working using quantitative metrics. They are different types of metrics. They can be used to get the appropriate types of questions to the customer.

Naturally, each methods come with other features beneath them, which make them more user-friendly. You'll notice that both of these methods come with useful and vanity metrics.

These types of metrics are not likely to result in changing the way you think about the subject matter you're worried about. They are a huge waste of time and should be avoided these as much as you can. They appear to offer you good guidance and advice that you can take action on however, they rarely take you to the right place and create more problems. If you're working with a business to assist you in determining your metrics, you should be careful when they tout the benefits of using one of the vanity metrics.

The use of actionable metrics will change the way that the thing operates that you're worried about. These are the kinds of metrics you need to use in your project. These are the metrics that will help you determine the strategy that you must follow, and help you to develop ways to make your company more efficient.

The reporting of metrics is an excellent method of determining how the company is doing when it comes to everything from everyday tasks.

Analytical metrics can help you uncover the facts you may not know about your business.

Lagging metrics are a good thing to consider in situations where you require more an overview of the company and you need as much information as you can to assist in making a choice. The churn rate of a company can be an excellent illustration of slow-moving metrics. This is due to the fact that it is going to tell you the number of customers who have cancelled their orders after a particular period of time.

Leading metrics are beneficial because they give you the data necessary to develop forecasts for the future of your business. Customer complaints are an excellent example of leading metrics since it will allow you predict the way a client will respond.

It is important to decide what kind of metric you would like to utilize based on the issue or project that you're working on. Utilizing one type of measurement is generally the ideal. It helps you stay in the right direction, so that you're aware of what you should be looking for. Do not waste time trying to tackle multiple metrics. It is only going to make you confused and leave with no understanding of the best strategy to follow.

What are the benefits of metrics?

So, take a look at John's tale again. We all know, it is your goal to earn a profit but when that doesn't succeed or just takes some time (even when you thought you could do it) you start to worry and angry with yourself. You may choose to leave. It's crucial to realize that the significance of measuring metrics is not overstated.

Metrics can give you an edge over seemingly insignificant events that can cause your company to be bankrupt.

To get the most value out of your metrics Here are some tips and some benefits

Take the following steps to ensure that you follow them: Metrics offer numerous advantages but first you have to adhere to the steps, and you must first decide on the data you want to track. Making the right choice of metrics involves certain processes, which include:

Establish your company's goals for the governing purpose The saying goes that "when the purpose of something isn't recognized, it is a given that abuse will occur". To accurately determine what you should be tracking the goals of your business, they must be defined clearly, and without which you'll continue to go around in circles, and it could become very frustrating. It could appear as if you're doing many hours and making only a tiny amount of advancement.

Find out what is the key to your business's success. You must be aware of the factors that allow you to progress and be successful, as that will help you decide what areas to invest greater effort in. For certain companies they are the clients and this means that they have to offer top-quality services and maintain an excellent relationship between the customer and marketer which will increase the customer feedback which will benefit your the business.

What can employees do to achieve the goals of the organization Once the goals are defined it is essential to define what that each employee should do to accomplish these objectives and if they are laid out specifically for every employee, it will make it less likely that employees don't understand the specifics of their job i.e. the employee isn't aware of what is expected of him at any given moment.

Re-evaluation of statistics; regularly, statistics must be evaluated to see if the company's goals are in line with the actions of the employee. It should be reviewed each one month, or at least every two weeks, to be sure that the proper activities are carried out.

Causality and Convenience If causality can be proved beyond doubt, and it is accessible easily for the tracking of progress between employees and employers this is an advantage. When the analysis has identified key elements that are crucial to successful outcomes and is completed, everything is in place and everything is in order. If the impact of a specific marketing campaign is something that needs to be evaluated, identify and understand how the products impact the overall bottom line versus your usual method. If the same-product sales can be a good indicator of growth in revenue, make sure to take action. The dashboard method is employed often for tracking purposes It gives you an instant review of the data that "call on the balls" This approach is more effective as it takes the pressure of having to read the entire report or specific complicated spreadsheet several times. If this method is implemented, you must match your business's and objectives to what's expected. A one-size-fits-all approach will not work for your particular business for this particular situation as errors can be made, which can be detrimental to the business.

Make sure you are careful If you are able to make the right choice, the benefits are numerous; resources and employees will be pushed towards goals that will increase business growth and the measures that are pursued will be based on company objectives, employee pay will not be taken over and the numbers won't be the main focus since measurements will reveal the exact condition of the company whether it's doing well or not, and not the extent to which employees are able to figure out what the company is searching for, and therefore aren't able to alter the data to meet their own needs. For instance someone who is aware that decisions are made based by yearly volume may choose to make an order one day before the period of reporting with understanding that the order could be delayed or cancelled in order to increase figures. This won't happen since metrics will show the state in which the business is.

Data must decidethat Metrics should be utilized to your advantage when they are of great use for your company. Metrics won't exist, and if you put the burden of "knowledge" on top of it. but you have to let the data decide. For instance, you might think that the amount of visitors visiting your site is equivalent to the amount of revenue you make in a day. If the metrics don't support that it is however, it's not true and never will be. If metrics are present they should serve as the indicator of the growth and development of your business. This way you will make the most profit and minimize stress.

Don't waste time and money on incorrect things: Once you choose to focus on the important things, you can take away the stress of other and irrelevant things. With measurements, and it provides you with an easy path to get.

- Helps you prioritize your tasks If you're not able to find time to do the small but important things. Metrics can help you organize your tasks accurately and easily. With metrics, you'll know precisely what you need to do to achieve the most effective outcomes.

The next thing you do is throw the metrics?

We are all aware that anything that has an advantage is also a disadvantage; the objective is to determine which is superior to the other. Water is essential to the development in the human body. it's also necessary to satisfy the needs of daily life of mankind, that is everyone needs to take a bath or wash our dishes, cook, etc. If there's a flood there is still water however this time it could be devastating for those affected. Homes could be ripped into pieces, rivers will overflow and the river banks would overflow. This doesn't mean that water is bad, but it is having the right amount which is the most important thing. Similar can be said regarding metrics. Can they be utilized to gain an advantage? But, will they also be a source of negatives? Yes.

There are a variety of metrics, and all utilize numbers and economic concepts to describe business performance. Every business metric has disadvantages, and if they are not as they're constructed, it's in the way analysts may misuse them, thus giving inaccurate outcomes.

The drawbacks of metrics are but aren't included in;

Specificity: The level of precision that certain business metrics are defined could be a drawback. Data on security to generate a result can be helpful in gaining knowledge about a specific area of business , but will likely overlook other aspects and relegates them to the background and being considered to be unimportant. For instance the market position will reveal the proportion of a market is controlled by a particular company through sales. as a gauge or a marker of general stability this is not a great measure of metric analysis because it doesn't reveal the potential for growth in the industry or whether the business is competing in multiple markets simultaneously. A lot of focus on one area can result in other aspects being overlooked, which can cause a lot of harm to businesses.

Inaccuracy: The aim for business metrics to dissect the complicated realities of various aspects of an organisation's existence into tiny bits of information that are easily understood as well as recorded and evaluated against previous or subsequent information. Some metrics come with the risk of not being accurate which makes them extremely risky to employ when there's money to be sought or increases doubts about the results, instead of being used to dispel. This is especially the case for metrics that are based on estimates or forecasts. Forecasts based on research or the past performance, may be derived from a static budget of a company and could appear to be sound financial data, but when the actual data is actually inserted from analysts may be an enormous increase in the growth of industry as due to incorrect assumptions that were previously used to determine areas such as inflation, expenses, and so on.

Over-reliance: When it comes to evaluation of performance for specific measures like profit and loss statements, cash asset ratio can be relied on too much and ultimately may be completely incorrect. Since these metrics have merit, an impression is also created that other metrics are of little or nothing, and aren't as reliable , and therefore cannot be relied upon. The obligation to evaluate business-related metrics in their context and what the metrics indicate is placed solely to individuals. What other metrics show and how data works together to reveal an insight into a company is also dependent on the perceptions individuals think of them.

Untrue numbers: When metrics are not used correctly and are not aligned with your goals, or do not be able to achieve the desired impact in the end, this will be a negative. They must be predictive and constant to be effective, as well as regular comparison of metrics with the intended outcome. If a lot of emphasis is placed on measures that do not ensure any improvement in your goals and strategic objectives as well as the mission of your business this means you're heading the wrong direction.

If you're also evaluating the events that happen due to pure luck and take these to be indicators of future success you're in danger of falling into a rut and will fail sooner or later. A man who lives in a region where the weather is cool and cool during September, and the sales of umbrellas is fair, and during the month of March, the hottest and there's an election and the political party that is involved uses umbrellas as a strategy for campaigning It's not right to directly link his huge sales of umbrellas in march with the political campaign, and ignoring the weather conditions, as the latter would later discover it wasn't as successful as anticipated and that the metric put on the table was not effective.

The ability to alter your metrics is a big plus. your metrics are easily manipulable, it will be detrimental to the growth of your company. If employees learn that, as a radio host you're aiming to increase listeners' numbers and they might ask friends to note fake names, register, and then unsubscribe in a matter of minutes. It is essential to look at metrics which are secure and won't be altered. A superficial metric is not man's best friend.

Conflicting goals: When your interests are not considered, and your employees are careless are, they will take the opposite approach, and negative consequences can occur. If the motives of the employer is different from the interests from the employees, conflicts will be inevitable. If an employee's performance is judged by the quantity of items sold, he may try to evade the system by inviting "customers" to purchase the items in order to be appropriately compensated, provided they will return the items earlier or later.

Your metrics aren't you It is crucial to not get stuck in the trap of thinking that you are your own metrics. You are the only human being in the business world, and it is full of lows and highs and there are times when you're in the middle. While it is essential to monitor your performance metrics, you should not connect your value to numbers, as it could make you feel emotionally ill. When your metrics don't appear to be of high quality because we humans are influenced by our emotions and thoughts, and this can result in unexamined behavior by the participants.

Human factor: Metrics may cause you to overlook human factors, and all you can do is be focussed on numbers. In the event that human issues are the reason for the decline in the business it's not necessary to focus on numbers. The human aspects should be fixed. are employees content and do they get enough sleep, or are they exhausted? Human factors are as crucial as numbers and data but don't put one over the other.

vanity metrics: These are the metrics of social media's engagement share, page views. While they do not have a significance to your financial results but they may be a source of happiness and who wouldn't want some extra motivation by something similar to that and the boost in morale it provides could boost your team. The obsession with metrics can reduce this. Be aware of the "pointless" number.

Chapter 7: Social Media Marketing

In the past, I've frequently mentioned the significance of using social media for marketing. It is worthy of a area of its own that will be covered in the coming two sessions.

We're at one of the best communications opportunities ever seen thanks to the wide array of channels for marketing on social networks available at the fingertips of entrepreneurs.

In this article, we will look at Facebook, Twitter, LinkedIn Pinterest, Instagram and YouTube in depth, so that by the end of the article, you'll be able to understand how and why you should use each of these channels to your company.

Beginning with Facebook. It is possibly one of the most-loved social media platforms.

Most likely, we have a Facebook profile to share information with your family members and acquaintances.

Social Media Marketing

However, let's make it certain, we're talking about a corporate Facebook profile and it is a completely different.

In an investigation of 100 of the most popular companies that was conducted by Interbrand they discovered that 97% of the brands have Facebook pages. Facebook is home to 1.35 billion daily active users.

It is necessary to be here. However, a word of caution. Be sure to capitalize from your initial market study. Now you should have a clear understanding of your ideal market, their requirements and aspirations. You know the factors that drive them and the triggers that drive them to buy. You have uncovered the reasons why people purchase products or services from you. This is the information you need to incorporate to Facebook posts. Facebook posts.

The secret isn't to sell directly via Facebook but rather to generate an interest by releasing relevant announcements that advertise your business.

Facebook is extremely effective in connecting us. You might want to think about forming the creation of a closed user group for your company or subject of your interest.

audiences

- Facebook profile
- Mass market
- Business v Personal
- Announcements/PR
- Advertising
- Digital breadcumbs

Find me on
facebook

Facebook advertising is easy focused and inexpensive however I'm not sure the effectiveness of it in creating sales. It all depends on your goals for this particular channel.

Interest in high volume is a must and customer engagement is a plus. PR yes , but direct sales is unlikely. My advice is to be specific about what you intend to accomplish via Facebook.

LinkedIn is a widely-used social media platform. The profile of a user on LinkedIn is different from Facebook. LinkedIn is designed for professionals and not for users from the public. You must create a an online presence that is professional.

This requires a professional head and shoulders photo. It's not the one you took during your holiday snaps. It is easy to create on your phone, or you can request a friend to shoot one or a series of photos, but it should be taken against an unlit light or white walls. And please make sure to smile and wear a professional attire. But , let's not take the unprofessional picture, Please.

The reach of LinkedIn for professionals LinkedIn is quite astonishing. LinkedIn is the primary source for HR professionals, however for entrepreneurs it could bring in new business opportunities.

Consider LinkedIn as your initial contact list for business that is new to you. LinkedIn is not only for your existing connections but the influence of who your leads are and who leads of your leads are aware of.

Reach of LinkedIn is staggering. As an example, I have approximately 1500 LinkedIn contacts, however within those contacts , those individuals have 13m connected users, meaning they're completely within my reach. Take a moment to digest those numbers. the fact that my 1500 contacts give me into 13 million. Quite staggering.

audiences

- Professionals
- Reaching decision makers

Linked in

- Targeted connections
- Lead generation
- Quality content
- Avoid the hard sell

If I'm trying to get in touch with the Chief Executive or the decision person of a company, I investigate whether they are connected to one people I have in contact with. I check who familiar with whom. The next step is writing an LinkedIn note to the contact, asking for an introduction.

The most important thing to remember is to make sure you give them a reciprocal offer. I refer to it as "givers get". It is a great way to earn dividends. If you've got a connection, you can send an immediate message to them directly. Do not use a direct sales pitch and instead frame the message in the manner of I'd also like to help.

A consistent and quality post is essential for success on LinkedIn But, be clear on the goals you wish to achieve via this platform.

It is no doubt that social media is a potent marketing tool for entrepreneurs. Every opportunity must be seized.

YouTube is an effective marketing channel. With over 1 billion users, the video-sharing giant, which is owned by Google gives you fantastic opportunities to make simple content in an fascinating ways to present and promote your company.

My suggestions here are to pay attention to the viewer's attention span. There is a trend to keep content short and succinct. Two or three minute video clips can be extremely appealing. The longer clips of 10 minutes could be boring.

As always, quality content is essential. With high-definition videos taken via your phone or camera, as well as easy-to-use editing software, you can create innovative video content.

The process of creating a YouTube channel is quite simple and provides an excellent platform for promoting your company.

My main tips here are to provide an attractive thumbnail image of your video. Don't just following the suggestions of others, and instead develop your own. Also, make sure that you have an opportunity to engage viewers in your video, for example the option to like or request a comment.

audiences

- Complementary
- New medium
- Quality & content
- Channel – series
- Thumbnails
- Call to action

You Tube

You can try the video editor software, such as iMovie or Camtasia which will increase the professional look and feel of your video.

Pinterest is an extremely popular channel that is rapidly growing. If you look at the users of the profile with 70 million+ users, they're mostly females educated, wealthy, and parents, and live in cities within the US. Europe is slow to adopt Pinterest however, you can be the first to adopt it and create new patterns of use. It is evident that Pinterest users are innovative and tend to spend a lot of money buying the item they are pinning about. Food is by far the most popular subject that is pinned. If you're in the restaurant industry or in an experience food, this can be an effective way to connect with you.

audiences

- Emerging channel
- Users, mostly women, educated, creative mothers
- Inspirational
- Monitor competition
- Pin regularly

Pinterest

Because Pins are a major driver of purchases for consumers, they are a good place for you to grow. Pins are a reflection of what we enjoy represent our dreams and desires, and thus can be effective marketing channels.

I have a customer who produces rucksacks, and she promotes her business on Pinterest and these translate in actual sales. Similar to my jewellery customer, my client makes use of Pinterest to draw attention to her jewelry designs, which can increase sales.

The main message is to come up with plans, understand your market, and pin the items they'll be looking for.

Twitter has more than 288m active monthly users. As such, it has a huge audience. However, unlike Pinterest which is a social network, Twitter serves an entirely different goal.

Twitter offers users opportunities to engage in conversations, sparking discussions, usually small, but sometimes a powerful tool to promote.

Examine the areas where you would like to create an identity and then search for individuals to follow. It is crucial to spend time researching who, what your area of expertise is and what you would like to share. Find out what are the factors that influence your market.

Twitter is a fast and simple way to express your opinion and be noticed. Don't be expecting to sell on Twitter but instead create your own social media presence on the most important subjects you wish to be recognized for.

My advice is to encourage you to use RT (retweet) requests on the top of the tweet. It is a way to ask your network to endorse your content.

If your message is important and relevant, they're likely to be willing to distribute your message to their networks and so on. I suggest using hash tags as well as images in your toolkit for Twitter promotion, since they are efficient.

Beware of the typical errors of tweeting "I'm at an establishment with buddies' '... or making derogatory remarks regarding individuals. One of my unreliable interns posted on Twitter that she was miserable at her job, and then rant about what she thought of her boss. It was obvious that it was noticed by the company and she was dismissed. My advice is to be cautious about the content you share. Think about it and consider what you would like it to accomplish.

Images are the main thing on Instagram. The photo sharing network that has more than 200 million active users sharing photos and videos is a efficient marketing channel. A majority of the top 100 brands utilize it. It is a good idea to do the same.

If image is a key aspect of your company I have some ideas.

I recommend that you invest your time to make use of this avenue. Find out the optimal dimensions and the definition of images to upload, then design your content with care, work out the most effective timing to publish, and then choose an analytics tool that can monitor your performance. Utilize hash tags to ensure your images and videos noticed.

The smart social media marketer will seamlessly post on Instagram, Facebook and Twitter but first determine to determine how they are noticed.

An effective tool to make effective utilization of the social media marketing channels is social media aggregators. That means, tools to spread your content across various channels, and to look up key phrases and possibly what people are talking about your company. Take a look at Hoot Suite or the Tweet Deck.

Instagram

- Photosharing network
- Image and video
- Top brands
- Analyse
- Hashtags
- Cross post

Instagram

In the end, we've only a handful of the tools for marketing on social media. The list is endless, but Facebook, LinkedIn, Twitter, YouTube, Pinterest and Instagram are my personal favorites. the primary tools.

They should be an element of your marketing strategy. It is important to figure out what you would like to accomplish through social media marketing, and how you plan to go through it.

Choose to focus on quality instead of the quantity. Marketing efforts must have a purpose and not just be random.

Activity 6

Social media marketing strategy

The next step is to take a look at your word document or notebook. In a new document begin to select the social media platforms you intend to utilize. For each, write down your goal for each channel , and then write down the steps you plan to take to accomplish each goal.

Begin with a concise paragraph or a series of bullet points about how you intend to utilize each, and most importantly , why you do:

Facebook

LinkedIn

YouTube

Pinterest

Twitter

Instagram

This is the next stage in preparing your business strategy.

Chapter 8: Establishing Your

Crowdfunding Campaign

Let's examine the details of the three phases discussed in the previous paragraphs. There are many things to keep in mind and there are instances when you might have missed something during the process. That's where crowdfunding consultants come to help. They can assist you in setting the foundation and guide through the whole procedure.

Before you begin the process of raising money it is essential to clarify what the goal is. As you will need to persuade and convince people to donate the money they've earned it is essential to give them the right information about the goals you wish to accomplish. Be truthful about your goal Naturally but don't exaggerate everything.

If you're selling a product you're selling, it's better if you have a prototype or sample which you could show prospective investors. This will give them an idea of what you're going to make and how beneficial it would be for them, and whether is worth the time and money they're investing in the project.

The projects that get funded fast are ones that provide something unique or useful for the consumer. If you're only looking for the money, it's likely that your product won't be successful. An idea that's good can only get you to the point of success if you don't have the resources is required to prove it the idea will be a waste of time.

What are some of the essential points you need to outline prior to starting an online crowdfunding campaign? Here's the information you should remember:

Define your project's idea clearly the scope, its purpose and timeframe.

Examine the feasibility and viability of your concept. You must come up with something that is useful to the people. If you're able to bring something unique on the market, it's all the better.

Make sure you research your market. Research similar projects and consider what they could be improved.

Be aware of any regulations and standards which could impact your venture. For instance, if you're planning to develop skincare products you should check various laws related to cosmetics that are available in the United States, such as the FPLA or Fair Packaging and Labeling Act and the FD&C or the Federal Food, Drug, and Cosmetic Act.

Create samples of your product. You will have to spend money on properly presenting your product. It must appear professional and nearly identical to the product itself.

Check your prototypes to determine whether your product actually works. This is crucial when you have prototypes available. If there's something that's wrong with the product, or it's not functioning as you would like Revision and review it.

Make sure you know the way you intend to use the money that you raised through crowdsourcing. Will you make the final product? Will you make use of it to expand? Do you plan to use it to purchase equipment for production?

Why is this so important? It ensures investors that you have a clear vision about the goals you're trying to reach. It's not uncommon to have projects fail while attracting a large number of investors. In reality, there have been numerous instances where entrepreneurs failed to live up to the promises they stated, which could leave their reputation and their business affected. Let's take this company as an instance:

In the year 2015, Torquing Group Limited has launched a campaign on crowdfunding to fund a small drone named Zano. After the company raised over 2 million dollars of capital but the project was scuttled off due to the fact that Zano was not as effective as they had believed it would be. Zano was a disaster.

A total of twelve thousand and two hundred contributed to the project, and about three thousand have pre-ordered the item. Out of that 600 got an actual product. Torquing offered features they couldn't deliver: panoramic thermal imaging cameras, high-definition video recording and audio recording built-in.

The company used all the money raised to hire software engineers, firmware experts, developers of websites and even marketers. While there is no evidence to suggest that Torquing attempted to defraud donors, the 12 thousand who donated money for the project are dissatisfied.

This is the reason you need to make clear what your product's purpose is. Don't make promises that are unable to provide. If you make promises that you can't deliver you'll lose credibility as an owner.

The best moment to start an appeal for crowdfunding?

A crowdfunding campaign typically lasts between thirty and 90 days. Therefore, it's recommended to start a campaign around 6 months (or earlier) prior to the launch date. When your item is seasonal that is, it's best at a specific season and you want to start your campaign six months prior to that. This gives you enough time to introduce the product and take it on the market before the season arrives.

It is possible to look over the pre-campaign to be able to test the waters before you actually launch your crowdfunding campaign. There are websites and services which allow you to design an online page to announce the intention to launch an online crowdfunding campaign.

This is the Pre-Crowfunding Campaign Checklist

Here's a list with essential things to consider prior to launching the pre-crowdfunding process.

Create a website or an online landing page.

The idea is to release the announcement in order to inform people about the possibility. If you're creating an organic acne product, for instance you can share images of your products in your web site. It is also possible to include details of the product - ingredients and benefits, as well as the process of making it, etc.

Make use of your website for business to convey your story and sell your product. It should load quickly and looks appealing for mobile phones. Additionally, you should include an "call for act" content that will encourage the visitors of your site to contribute to your crowdfunding campaign. It is also recommended to add "behind behind the scenes" images. In this way, potential donors will get to know your organization a bit more.

Create an all-star campaign team.

A crowdfunding campaign run by a group earns over three times more than crowdfunding campaigns run by individual contributors. This is due to the fact that working as the team expands your networks which increases the potential reach that your project can reach. A team allows you to concentrate on the areas you're proficient in. Your team members on crowdfunding aren't necessarily your employees. They could be colleagues or family members, your friends or anyone you trust.

In addition to the team that will assist you in managing your crowdfunding website. It's also possible contact people who can assist you with your product photos as well as graphic design and pitch videos. Of course, you could complete these tasks on your own. However using the services of an experienced photographer or graphic artist could help you save a lot of time, and also to reduce the burden. You can also be sure that you'll get high-quality , professional-looking work.

Make an email list.

After you've written your pitch's pitch video, text as well as a plan for the project and budget, you'll be required to collect email addresses and construct your list of mailing addresses. The list of email addresses you collect will include those from prospective customers as well as any other parties interested who agree to let others know about your campaign via social media, and other channels once you've launched it.

Use these suggestions when creating your mailing list:

Take business cards when you go to networking events, make sure you ask for the business cards of people. This will allow you to create your list of mailing addresses.

Sign up sheets are a great way to get people on board. when you exhibit your products at a trade fair and you are exhibiting, ask your visitors to put their email addresses and names on a sign-up form.

Invite visitors to sign up with their email addresses - You can offer an ebook for free for the exchange of email address.

It is important to note that you are not yet looking for investors What you're seeking are people who will present your investment plan to the public. The typical time frame for pre-campaigns is between 60 and 90 days. This is how long you will need to create the message of your marketing campaign. The more email addresses you have in your email list, more likely you are to have the success.

The Accounting and Tax Costs and all the Legal Matters

While you're putting the finishing touches on your project, it's important to be aware of the legal and tax issues prior to launching your crowdfunding campaign. If you don't have an account for your business and you're not sure where to start, you should open one. This is the time when your CPA can be a huge aid to you. It is also important to establish either an LLC, or limited liability corporation. Establishing a company prior to when you start the crowdfunding campaign can boost the credibility of your campaign.

Here are some steps you need to take to make your venture an actual company:

Select the name for your LLC.

Create the "articles of organisation". The requirements differ from state to state.

Make sure you pay the filing fees. The fee is usually approximately $100. Additionally, you must pay an annual tax in addition to the filing costs.

Make an LLC operating contract.

Put a notice on the local newspaper. Certain states require this.

Find permits and licenses.

Additionally, you should obtain legal advice when dealing with the following matters:

Tax. The income you get from rewards and pre-sales could be tax-exempt. It is possible to consult a tax professional or an accountant with experience to assist you get tax deductions and exemptions, in the event that there are any.

Intellectual Property. Many entrepreneurs were sued due to the fact that they used copyrighted images and videos with no permission. For instance, Ultra sued Michelle Phan for using Kaskade's songs without permission. Be aware that there are many shady entrepreneurs who copy ideas from crowdfunding campaigns that are on Kickstarter as well as Indiegogo.

Before you begin your campaign, it is important to create an outline of all the expenditures related to the project and record all contributions. This can be done by yourself in the case of just a couple of thousand dollars. However If you're planning on fundraising more than 10 thousand dollars. It's a good idea seek assistance by an accountant.

Chapter 9: Your Startup Idea

There are numerous types of businesses that you can set up However, certain types are sought-after as start-ups. The benefit of creating your own company is that you have numerous industries to pick. Every type of business comes with its pros and drawbacks. Some, like sales businesses, will require more experience than other businesses before you are able to make a profit. Some businesses require little or none of capital and others require significant capital upfront. But, with the right amount of enthusiasm and determination you can establish an income-producing business in any sector.

Basic Business Types

Retail businesses typically have stores to sell their items. Some examples of businesses that are retail include book stores, clothing boutiques, jewel stores cell phone stores and so on. Retail businesses may also operate through online shopfronts. There are numerous methods to create your own storefront online using platforms like PayPal as well as Shopify. You can also offer sales through an online storefront operated by a third party like Craigslist as well as eBay.

Wholesale companies allow customers to purchase large amounts of goods directly from the manufacturers and sell them to small retail stores. For instance wholesalers may offer the same soda products to a local grocery retailer or a particular variety of pastry products to restaurants. They later turn around and sell their products for their clients.

Franchises are what you get when you purchase a licence to market services or products belonging to an established company. Fast-food eateries are a well-known kind of franchise. Entrepreneurs often purchase the restaurants of one franchise, so that they can open at many locations. Although franchises can be extremely profitable and very effective, franchise owners are required to make payments for franchisor fees as well as royalty to the franchisor, and comply with the specific guidelines stipulated by the franchising company.

Services-focused businesses are appealing for startups because they don't require as much funding for their launch like other types of businesses. You are often able to be self-employed when you're an expert in the field you are interested in. Writing, construction, and financial advice are just a few of the most well-known service-based business models. Expert professionals such as dentists, doctors as well as lawyers, are thought of as service companies. Sometime, a business that is specialized in a particular service will also fall under this category of sales. For instance, a dental office might sell top-of-the-line dental toothbrushes on sale, as well as offering dental services.

Digital companies are popular as entrepreneurs because they typically have the smallest amount to start , and need less than the access to a computer with internet connectivity. A lot of freelance businesses fall in this category. Any service that is performed remotely is classified as a digital business.

The assembly-based service can also be excellent startups. In this type of company the person or group of people subcontracts projects from larger manufacturing firms. They can assemble, pack or other ways to make a product already available to be sold at the end of the day.

Companies which sell clothing or makeup products through trusted companies such as Avon as well as Posh are a different option for startup companies. Your range of products and the people you intend to sell them to could be restricted by the kind the product that you're selling. If you're adept at crafts and arts making your own products, selling them could be a viable option. Many craftsmen and artists sell personalized mugs, tshirts, jewelry, and more through brick-and mortar and online selling platforms.

It is important to remember that a startup or is a company that offers an entirely new product or one that provides an existing service or product in a completely new manner. It's crucial to stay clear of duplicateing an already-existing business concept. Your business idea should be distinct enough from other ideas in the market to qualify as a unique concept.

What is your industry?

It is simply a method to categorize your company. There are a variety of reasons why to know the specifics of your industry. The first is that it provides you with an industry profile to assist in defining your business's place within the industry. A profile for the industry will provide important details on the market that you're entering. It provides the forecast for what direction your particular business is expected to be in the near future. This data will assist you in making intelligent decisions regarding the feasibility of your business concept. Before you decide to pursue this particular idea you should investigate the relevant industry to determine whether the idea is worth the effort.

The listing of industries is pretty typical. The major categories include:

Businesses in agriculture.

Business services.

Consumer service businesses.

Education-based businesses.

Utilities and energy businesses.

Entertainment companies.

Financial-based businesses.

Healthcare-based businesses.

Manufacturing companies.

Non-profits.

Construction and real estate businesses.

Retail companies.

Technology-based businesses.

Telecommunications.

Transportation companies.

Travel businesses.

Wholesaling.

As an example an enterprise offering networking services is a part that includes business-related services. If you were to establish an auto-limousine company the industry you would work in will be transport. If you were to offer your jewelry that you made yourself, it would fall under the retail category.

After you've decided on your type of business then you'll need to study the specific field to determine whether your business idea is a good fit to be a success in its launch and long-term success within the industry.

Clarify Your Idea

After you've become acquainted with the industry you're interested in Next step is to define your startup concept If you don't have it yet. The possibilities for ideas for startups are limitless. It could take some effort and time to develop ideas that are original but the effort is worth it as all your research will only increase your knowledge of the chosen field.

Consider things that are trending particularly with regards to a technology-based business concept. As an example, you would not launch a company selling a new cassette player in 2017! If you were to create a video streaming service which also downloads videos onto your television and other devices, it might be a feasible possibility.

To stay on top of the current trending developments, you'll want to think about how the future of streaming services and TV technology will look like in the coming five or 10 years. You're seeking an idea that can be successful not just in today's marketplace but for the long run. It needs to be able be upgraded, changed and styled to match changes in the focus of industry and trends.

Which is Your Business Category?

If you've settled on your idea for a startup and you've done your research to assess its potential on the market, congrats you're one step ahead of the competition! You can skip this section.

If you've not come up with an effective concept, or need help analyzing the various elements of your company plan this section could assist. While you're unlikely to have an entirely developed idea in the blink of an eye Here are some industries that seem to be promising.

Explore what you are interested in and continue to work through it until you've developed your own unique venture idea

Software for application.

Box delivery businesses.

Cleaning services.

Coaching or consulting.

Handyman or contractor.

Electronics repair

Food-based ideas.

Freelancing.

Services for landscaping and gardening.

Nutrition and health services.

In-home services.

Instructor.

Services or products that are suitable for children.

Pet services.

Photography.

Researching.

Businesses using social media.

Tour guide.

Translation.

These are just a few ideas to get your imagination flowing. The possibilities for new ventures are limitless.

Start with Your Passions

Based on my own experience I've found that the most successful business concepts, come out of thin air. Additionally, some of the most innovative concepts are actually easy to implement! It's possible try playing with the "what-if" game by asking yourself questions that generate a fresh idea. Be alert while on the go and look for ways to improve your existing offerings or even services. Find the need that's waiting to be met.

Incorporate your interests and talents when brainstorming. If you can pinpoint your passion or talent and then find a way to fulfill your goal, you'll be more likely to achieve success and satisfaction as an business owner. It's much easier to achieve success when you're working in an area of interest and passion. When you're doing something that you enjoy and you are committed to it's much more motivating to wake up each day and continue to work until the reward is earned!

How Effective is Your Idea?

After you've developed an incredible startup concept You'll need to demonstrate that it is able to become profitable. Your brilliant idea may not be from its time. It could be that the investment requirements are too expensive today to turn it into an effective business.

It is important to check the viability of your concept. One of my friends had an idea of creating car windshields that become dark upon contact with sunlight. it's a concept similar to the idea of light-sensitive eyeglasses. But, he soon realized that it was too costly to make. Also, he realized that it would not be compatible with states with regulations against tinted windows on cars.

You might be wondering what you need to do to determine whether your idea for a business is viable. That's why we've got an feasibility analysis.

The Feasibility Report

One of the most effective methods to assess the feasibility of your fantastic idea is to conduct research and create a feasibility study. The feasibility report will give an outline of your business concept and outline the market. It will assist you in estimating the funds you'll require to transform your idea into a viable product. The report takes into account issues like whether you possess the abilities to bring your concept from a conceptual point to reality. The report will also identify any regulations from the government that might be a hindrance and describe the steps you is going to take to get around them.

This knowledge will allow you to be one step ahead of the pack when it's time to create your business plan. It can aid you when you begin to look into financing. We'll cover these topics in the next chapters, but for the moment you should be aware that a thorough well-researched and well-thought-out feasibility report is worth the effort. If the numbers match up and everything is in order then you'll be one step ahead when it's time to develop your final business plan.

When you begin the feasibility study, it's essential to outline your business plan. Highlight what makes it different from existing products. Then, you should list all of your first items and services, and in few sentences, explain each item in detail. After that, you'll be able to focus on the following sections of your report:

Know Your Market

In the section on markets in your report on feasibility you will need be able to respond to the following inquiries:

Do you see a need to my item or my services?

Does my analysis of my industry appear promising?

Who is my customer?

How can I increase my public?

What makes your product/service stand out the rest? Why would my intended market buyers want to purchase from me?

What are my competitions? What are their advantages over me? Do I benefit from their advantages?

What are other challenges to marketing I need to be aware of?

Your Financing Overview

In the finance section in your report on feasibility you must be asked to answer these questions

What amount of capital do I require in order to start this project off of the foundation?

How simple will it be to obtain capital?

What can I do to finance my company during the beginning of its growth?

How much are fixed expenses? What are my variable costs?

How many items or services per client can I anticipate selling?

Do I have the ability to earn a profit?

What will it cost me to grow the number of customers I have?

What is the price strategy for my product or services?

What is my forecast for sales? appear to be?

What is the likelihood of my return on my investment?

Other Factors to Consider

This part of your feasibility report will contain other factors that could can impact your financial performance. In this section, you should include details of the following:

Location.

Licenses and permits are required.

The rights to Intellectual Property.

Regulations and standards.

Skills and education that are essential.

The need for employment and availability.

The changing trends.

Anything else you think of to improve the potential of your venture.

Once you've completed the feasibility study, it's time to review it to yourself. Does the evidence show that your idea can overcome the obstacles and risks to make it profitable? Can it endure the tests of time?

If the information contained in this report suggests that it is likely to succeed then you've got a feasible business concept in your hand! If you find that something isn't quite right with the data or they don't show the potential for growth You may have modify your concept or pick a different idea entirely.

Chapter 10: Additional Methods

Solutions to Probleme

This is a popular method of generating ideas. It is based on identifying the issue people are facing every day and providing them with products or services to solve these issues. The best method to attain this kind of thinking is to be aware of any issue that you are facing every day, instead of making excuses or dismissing the issue, consider it as an opportunity to grow your business. If you're going through this yourself, it's likely that other people have the same experience.

Be consistent about this. If you're putting in more effort than you need to complete every task (idea opportunity to generate revenue for the provision of a service) or if an item you bought does not work as you'd like it to (idea opportunity for generation for the product) be aware of the issue. What is the reason you aren't getting the value for your money? What can you do to fix it? The most important thing is to first understand the issue before attempting to resolve it. If you know the issue then you will be able to generate fantastic ideas with any method I've discussed throughout this publication.

Below are a few examples of concepts that can solve problems. I chose these examples because they appear to are tiny inventions, however they originated from typical problems people confront. If you can make people's lives easier by any means, then no idea will be considered too huge or small. It is your right to check out the videos and discover what issues these inventions address.

You'll never lose your wallet ever again:

https://www.kickstarter.com/projects/mijl o/wheres-wallet-the-smart-wallet-youll-never-lose?ref=category

Magnetic paper:

https://www.kickstarter.com/projects/tesl aamazing/magnetic-paper-that-sticks-to-walls?ref=category

Beehive picture hangers:

https://www.kickstarter.com/projects/100 5351285/beehive-picture-hangers?ref=category

Idea generation for the consumer

The idea generation process involves contact with the customer through surveys that determine the any setbacks to existing items or products (those that are part of the competition). For this, design surveys that contain questions that are designed to collect details about what consumers would like from service or manufacturer suppliers. It is possible to use open-ended questions, such as: what do you think this product could be improved? Do you feel satisfied with the service you received? What other things do you want service providers to accomplish?

The results will be extremely useful in coming up with concepts and is based on reliable evidence, which will eliminate the requirement to conduct an additional market survey since your service or product design will be based on real opinions of the customers initially.

Copying ideas

You could always make use of one of the well-known startup ideas. This type of thinking is focused on gaining a share of the pie, rather than creating a niche market. This is especially useful in the case of having a limited budget to begin your business and want to reduce the risk.

Remember that copying ideas do not involve using patents on intellectual property or other copyrighted materials or copying the structure of companies that have been profitable over time. Follow the law, but benefit from the practices of other companies.

Making as a pastime

Take a look at your talents and the hobbies you are interested in doing in your daily life. If you have a great knowledge about a specific passion, why not put your knowledge and experience into a profitable business? If, for instance, you are a guitar player with a great skill you could start an online tutoring company to teach others how to play cool jams and moves. You can draw on your expertise of your passion to earn money, or do things that complement your interest. For instance, if you enjoy fishing instead of instructing individuals on how to fish correctly it is possible to begin a business selling fishing gear and books on fishing.

Note down your hobbies , and then think about what kind of business you could start with the help of the information I've provided throughout this publication. You can employ any strategy you want to use including brainstorming, or the idea matrix, to develop an idea for a business that you are already doing as an interest in your day-to-day life. You can certainly argue that turning your pastime into a business can diminish the enjoyment that you have from your pastime. It's not the case, but it is the primary argument for those who are about to become entrepreneurs that opt to not turn their passions into an enterprise.

I would suggest considering giving this business opportunity a shot as it could allow you to be able to enjoy your passion even more. In the end, you'll make money from something you already enjoy which will give you that wonderful satisfaction knowing that you are able to be a part of something that you love to do.

Utilizing the waste

This is an unusual but highly effective way to come up with ideas. The benefit of using waste to create things is that waste is generally inexpensive as well as free allowing you to reduce the material cost to a minimum in the moment.

All you have to do is find things that people do not utilize and want to eliminate. It could involve some driving around, such as taking old car parts and letting them are lying in junkyards. Be aware of the cost since fuel costs may not be worth it when compared to the cost of buying new materials or parts. Remember that if you employ this strategy for your business concept the business will be viewed as eco-friendly and sustainable.

Improving

Improvement involves looking at the existing service or product in small increments and attempting to figure out ways to create the item or service in a way that it's more efficient and user-friendly. Reverse-engineering products is one of the best examples of this. Reverse-engineering involves purchasing the product of a competitor and then analyzing it piece-by-piece to identify opportunities for improvement.

Another possibility is to restore old furniture or even real estate (real estate flipping). Buy old items, make improvements to their condition and then sell them at a higher price.

New version of the product

It is possible to create a brand fresh version of an already existing item in two ways. There is the means to make an item or provide an option that is less expensive than competitors or you can include new and exciting features to existing products, or change the way in which the service is provided.

Reverse Thinking

This is particularly helpful if you're trying to come up with an idea through solving the problem. Instead of tackling the issue consider what might create new issues. This reverse-thinking approach will enable you to think differently in the event that you're ever stuck with a challenge you'd like to resolve but are unable to move forward.

Backwards Thinking

This approach is to think about the process of making rather than the final product. You should think about ways to avoid problems that could arise in the production process. Also consider ways you can improve the production process so you will have higher quality products to market.

Big ideas

Consider something that is tiny in size , turn it into a huge object , and then sell the items. A good example would be huge works of art for foyers at companies.

Thinking Small

It is a common method to launch new toys by toy makers such as miniature electronic helicopters or house models for kids, and building kit kits designed for adult children (such as planes, cars or ships of the 18th century) and so on. Consider all the amazing products that are huge in size, and then sell the miniature versions of them.

Combining ideas

Find two items and mix them. You can use lists to help you do this. Try different combinations and note the combinations until you truly like the idea, before delving into its potential. Sometimes the most brilliant ideas will appear to you, but at it is best to be looking for them constantly. It's an excellent exercise for your brain. Combining ideas is among the most popular method of generating ideas, however this doesn't mean it's not efficient. Indeed, you can come up with extremely exciting ideas using this. Like A bath tub that has a an audio system built into it.

Poor competition

It is a great way to generate concepts since we easily become frustrated by a product or service every day. When you face a challenge that is related to a product or service the product you are offered take a look at the bright side with businessperson's eyes. You will see that the issue you've endured could lead to an idea for a business. Consider what producers or sellers are doing wrong and how you could make it better?

The benefit of this kind of idea generation is that you are already aware of the weaknesses of the competitor from a customer's perspective standpoint. If you recognize the weak points of products or services that you are able to fix them through the possibility of coming up with fresh ideas for an improved product or service.

Learning to build on your the skills

You can transform a personal talent that you use for fun into a profitable business. For instance, if you enjoy fixing automobiles, you could start your own garage or run the repair of cars. The advantage of such a thing is you do not require initial training as you are doing something that you enjoy and are well-acquainted of.

Importing

Search for products sold in foreign markets and bring them in for a low cost. The most important things be aware of are the cost of shipping tax, the safety regulations of your country particularly if you are selling products that could be harmful to someone's health. Importing businesses is very lucrative If you've got good negotiation abilities and strive to keep the cost of the goods you buy to a minimum. Make sure you are looking for quality goods and purchase them at the lowest price you can.

The most lucrative method of doing this is to purchase something that is not available in a specific region but this can be difficult and there may be more buyers waiting to purchase what you're looking for. The reason why the product is not available in your area could be because there isn't any need for the product, and that other importers have realized that and have decided to steer clear of the business. For the US imports of textiles, it can be extremely profitable (check the other options that could be lucrative).

Exporting

Similar to that, you can also perform the exact opposite when you buy a good from home and then transfer it to other countries.

What do they have to do with what they are?

In the final instance, you may look at the functions of a product instead of the thing they're. For example scissors. Scissors can cut hair, paper, etc. Consider how you can accomplish this using a different product. This is a fantastic method of thinking outside the box, since the majority of people use scissors if they had for cutting paper.

Chapter 11: Making A Resume

"You should not be focusing on the reasons the reasons why you aren't able to do something that is what the majority of people do. Instead, you should think about what you can do and become one of the few exceptions."

Steve Case, Co-Founder and Co-Founder of AOL

If you're applying to the resume that you used to secure the job at your company or is the one that you will be giving out to companies both large and small, it is time to reconsider submitting it to any new jobs. A lot of people view an resume as just a listing of your previous work experience and duties but a start-up will want more than you have done in the past.

What should you include and what not to include on the resume?

The process of writing a resume can be an overwhelming job. There's a lot of details to be included and you only have a limited amount of space. The way you create your resume to submit to an employer is not the same as how you would like to write your resume when you are writing it for the start-up. While larger companies put greater importance on your professional experience while start-ups need to show outcomes. They don't want to simply know about your past work experience they need to know how your experience will affect your work at their organization. When you write your resume, you must consider particular items that you need to remove from your resume and other aspects you'll need to include to make your resume stand out.

What is not appropriate to include on your resume:

Image

If you're trying to find modeling, acting position you should include a photo but it is not the only reason it should be included on your resume. Included photos on your resume is not going to aid in getting the job. Often, resumes with pictures will be removed. The hiring managers and recruiters don't want to get accused of discrimination by including images on their resumes. Including your photos can cause some form of discrimination. You should also be selected based on your talents and skills, not due to your race, age or appearance.

Insignificant History

It is possible to think that including all the things you've done in the past will make your resume appear more impressive, but it can be detrimental. The inclusion of previous experience or achievements that do not have any effect on your ability to perform the task you'll be expected to complete is not a good idea and will not assist you in getting the job. In listing all of your previous experience is only required if the past experience proves to employers or recruiters that you are more in-depth or if the experiences have helped you to develop certain abilities or demonstrate your capability to perform in a specific manner that will be transferable to the job you're applying for.

Poor Formatting

The information you include in your resume neatly presented. While it is possible to include lots of information on the resume you submit, this may result in over-sizing and may be seen as being excessive. It is recommended to keep your experience, qualifications as well as descriptions, skills, and qualifications clear and to the main point. Make sure to leave space for white space, which makes it easier to understand.

Bullets are often used on resumes but you should make sure you convey crucial information you need to pay attention to. Don't use bullets on every aspect of your resume because this is likely to make the reader look over everything and can have the effect of highlighting items that are crucial.

Personal information is too personal

It is important to include your name as well as the best method of contacting you, as along with the email addresses. Other personal details such as multiple phone numbers, your mailing address, or the social security number should be removed from your resume. Although it was necessary to include these details on resumes in the past, these days, they pose security risks and, in many instances, not required by recruiters.

Lies

If you're trying to shine however, you shouldn't be a fraud on your resume. If they're attracted to your resume, they'll be conducting some research. If you are blatantly lying regarding your credentials, then you stand no chance of being successful in the startup industry. Falsely stating your resume's information is not only morally incorrect but it could cause you to be in a position you are not able to clearly be able to. If you are employed based on the assumption that you have specific skills that you aren't This could be harmful to the development of the company. Remember that the startup industry is a tight tied. If you've lied on your resume to gain an internship at one startup it is a high chance that other start-ups that you submit your application to and professionals from the industry will be aware of this, and the chances of getting into the business in the future are low to zero.

It's better to be honest about the abilities you are lacking however, you must also demonstrate a desire to discover what you do not have. This will add impact and increase chances of getting hired and staying in your job, rather than lying or not being completely open about things you don't fully understand or comprehend.

What should be included in your resume:

Keywords

The advancement in technology today makes it possible for recruiters to easily sort through resumes using pertinent information on resumes. Incorporating keywords into your resume will ensure that you are able to pass this initial screening process. The keywords you choose to include should match the position you're applying for, which isn't easy because the position you are applying for may not come with an explicit job description. The job advertisement will usually include a section that outlines the qualifications required, the skills needed or responsibilities , which could all be used as keywords. Keywords should be related to the abilities and capabilities that make you the perfect candidate for the position.

Also, you should utilize variations of keywords for example, using the words create and develop. To discover additional keywords, take a look at the business's "about me" page, and also look looking through the profiles of employees working there. Find out what words are employed to define the business and incorporate these phrases into your resume. If you go through profiles of the employees, take note of how each person describes themselves and the job they perform. That will enable you find the keywords you may want to include on your resume.

Keywords should be incorporated into your resume in each section. They should be relevant to the job you're seeking to fill, and also reflect the company branding. When you include these words in your resume, ensure to incorporate them in a manner that they are incorporated seamlessly into the resume without being excessively utilized.

Professional Acquired Skills

The abilities you've gained can be linked to your previous experiences. These could include educational experiences, internships, training, or projects that you've been involved in. The skills you've acquired can come from projects you've had as a participant in initiating or managing teams you've arranged. If you do only have some basic knowledge of a specific skill, it is sensible to list it on your resume. Understanding the basics is superior to having no knowledge at all, but should it not be mentioned in your application, the employer is unlikely to know what the difference is and conclude that you don't have these abilities.

Professional Links

Links to a professional and public profile could make it easier for recruiters to find out more about your profile. You should include an online link to your site, LinkedIn profile or other professional websites where your past work is visible. Links you add should be of only your professional activities, make certain that your skills and experience that are listed on the links correspond to those skills and experience listed on your resume. If there are photos that are included, they must represent you in a professional environment. Giving recruiters links to browse through will help them gain an understanding of what you can do and the value you provide.

Creating different resumes.

Although it's easier to submit the same resume to each job that you apply for, and in large corporations, this may be acceptable, this isn't an strategy you should take in your search for a startup. If you are applying to start-ups you should tailor every resume to that particular business.

Chronological resume

The chronological resume is likely one you've already created. It's the type of resume that concentrates on your work history and responsibilities at work. In this type of resume, you would include your work background from your most recent to the past. If you're experienced in making resumes and have a decent amount of experience it is the type of resume that you would typically present to an opening. It highlights your work experience and is a great way to demonstrate how the abilities that you've developed can be transferred to the job you're applying for.

What you'll want to be able to demonstrate a bit different when you apply to a start-up in comparison to a large business is to clearly demonstrate how you utilized your skills to achieve results. It's not enough to just list all the things you did at your current job. You must demonstrate how you could accomplish your task efficiently. If you were in charge of making weekly schedules and helped in this using software or an application which kept everyone informed of their work schedules and responsibilities, then you can claim that you were responsible for this.

Your resume should demonstrate your accomplishments and not just your work experience because recruiters and hiring managers for new companies are looking for proof that you'll be able produce outcomes. The fact that you have experience doesn't mean you're capable of, it indicates that you've been able to stay in a job which required you to perform specific things. It is important to emphasize the ways you improved and the new skills you gained and how that makes you a great candidate for the job you're seeking.

Experience and skills resume.

While employers prefer using a chronological format for resumes, it's not always the most effective format to utilize. If you're relatively new to the job market, you might not have a lot of work experience relevant to the job you're applying for. It could also be that you are undergoing an employment change that could make some of your previous employment history to seem insignificant. In any case you should consider putting your skills and experience on a resume could be better.

In this type of resume you will focus on your skills and the experiences you've acquired as well as other relevant details that informs the employer of your abilities.

The typical format is to not include your professional experience. This kind of resume could include any volunteer work you've done as well as internships, projects that you've been involved in as well as other ways that you've had the opportunity to build your skill set. In this type of resume, you'll want to showcase the abilities you've gained but also how you utilized these skills to achieve results or how they can be used in the job you're applying to produce results.

A resume of experience and skills should be well-organized. Include the most relevant abilities first, and then adding additional abilities later. It is important to demonstrate to the hiring manager and the recruiter that, even though you might not have the background for the job you're applying to but you have the essential skills needed to complete the job better than everyone else.

How do you highlight your accomplishments.

Be specific

You must have concrete results listed within your CV. Explain how the work you've accomplished in the past affected the companies you been employed at. Did you manage to complete a task far ahead of schedule? Write down these achievements and explain the length of time the project was completed. How did you increase profits and market penetration or cut down on production costs? Inform them of the amount.

Stop naming people

If you were employed by an enterprise of a large size even if it was an apprenticeship or only one-time job include the details. Find innovative ways to describe these highlights to demonstrate that you have the skills and motivation to use what you've got to obtain greater and more successful outcomes.

Be sure to be clear

Employers who are just starting out aren't likely to take a long time looking through and trying to figure out the entirety of your resume. If you are using jargon or other information that only your previous employer would be able to understand, you can rephrase it to make it easier for them to understand. If someone looking through your resume takes more than ten minutes to understand what you actually accomplished in the previous jobs, they'll simply leave.

Be flexible and show you are

A professionally organized resume is essential, however you shouldn't convey the impression that you're so rigid and ensconced in the guidelines that you will not be in a position to change and adapt according to the needs of work in a startup. You must demonstrate that you are able to manage the chaos in a systematic and efficient way. There's an important distinction between being concise and clear and being rigid enough that you are unable to quickly think and make changes to plans when the need arises for it. It is important to note that you have been in a position to assume different roles during times of crisis or when the plans you had in place required to change in the opposite direction.

Creating a cover letter

One of the biggest errors you can commit when you are submitting your resume to a start-up job is if you do not include the section of writing your cover letter. The decision to take this extra step can go an extremely long way to impress those making the hiring. A cover letter does not just show that you're willing to go that extra mile but is also one the most effective ways to demonstrate how you'd be a good fit for the company. Here are some tips to create an outstanding cover letter

If you're planning to claim that you have done things well, you must give examples of the reasons behind this. While you don't want to simply summarize your resume. Instead, you should make use of your cover letter to elaborate on the ways you have been able to perform the tasks you've done previously. Then, give them the outcome and then describe the process that led to the outcomes.

Make sure to include keywords throughout your cover letter too. One method to bring them to life is to include an alphabetized list within your body section of the letter. The bullets should highlight your accomplishments, and include the most relevant keywords.

Don't use the generic salutation, and learn the name of the hiring manager. When you begin your letter of cover, you should begin by adressing the person it's meant for. Most people will use an unspecific introduction, like " Dear Mr. or Mrs." and "To whomever it might concern." If you're in a position to identify an individual name for the person who is responsible for the hiring department, then send it to a specific job such as "Hiring manager of the marketing department." This can help create a more personal letter and easy to personalize.

Your cover letter should begin with a description of the job you're applying for and showing your enthusiasm for the job.

The first line in your letter of cover needs to draw the recruiter's or hiring manager's attention . get them interested in learning more about yourself and why you're so enthusiastic about the job you are applying for.

Be imaginative. Your creativity will help you get noticed and make you stand out. It is not necessary to adhere to the standard template of a cover-letter If you can come up with a more effective method of showcasing your abilities and your worth. Explore the possibilities and see what you could think of.

Keep it brief. Your cover letter needs to be short and to the point. it can be accomplished with just half of a page or a little more. Do not take up a whole page for writing your cover letter, unless you are using lists or bullet points.

Write the last words on your cover letter in order to highlight what you stand for and leave an impression that lasts. Don't just close your cover letter with a "hope that you will hear from me soon" or any other variation of this. Instead, you should use the last paragraph in your letter of cover to make clear what you can offer , as well as any additional information that proves your dedication.

Sending videos

One method to creatively write your covering letter to the employer is to make videos. It can be done in a variety different ways, and is a great way to showcase your character, passion in your work, abilities, and values. If you're seeking an opportunity as a marketing manager of a new start-up, an instructional video showing you can promote yourself is an effective way to demonstrate your abilities in a new manner. This is a good option for those changing career paths or moving from large corporate to the start-up sector. You'll want to stand out but you need to make it happen in a successful manner.

Don't simply put up a camera and speak in a monotone manner Think of ways you can demonstrate your abilities and character in a matter of two seconds or less. Demonstrate how you can apply your persuasive skills to convince your children to eat their broccoli and show how you can transform a messy workspace into an office that is fully functional or rally your colleagues and then give them a motivating talk to showcase your leadership abilities. There are many simple methods to display your talents in a unique way that can make potential employers keep you in mind.

It is also possible to use video clips to showcase your enthusiasm for the business or for the job you're applying to. Show them that you're willing to take risks. Demonstrate that you're able to break away from the standard approach to things and that you are prepared to explore new ideas.

Do not forget to keep in touch.

If you wish to prove that you're truly keen on the job it is important to follow-up. Give it a few days to wait and then follow up with an by phone or email if you applied. This again indicates your enthusiasm for the job, and could be a major factor in whether you are invited for interviews or not.

Conclusion

I'm hoping you're now in a position to take major steps to make your business goals become a realisation.

Be creative and determined. Always ready to pursue your goals Take calculated risks, and be capable of planning and delegating. There are a variety of industries around the world where it is possible to start a business. It is based on the concept the startup will require no or little investment while others require substantial investment. Because there are a variety of sectors to choose from, it's essential to study your idea thoroughly to determine if there is demand for it and if it's financially viable.